FAST FOOD

MOSES

BIBLE CHARACTER STUDIES
FOR PRE-TEENS

BY DARREN

First published in 1998 by
KEVIN MAYHEW LTD
Rattlesden
Bury St Edmunds
Suffolk IP30 0SZ

© 1998 Darren

0 1 2 3 4 5 6 7 8 9

ISBN 1 84003 255 3
Catalogue No 1500216

Cover by Darren
Edited by David Gatward
Printed in Great Britain

Contents

FAST FOOD SERIES

JOSEPH
PETER
DAVID
MOSES

Look out for further titles

Introduction

When it came to researching these character studies I was suddenly struck by how patchy my knowledge of them actually was! I knew the well-known stories but rarely as much as I thought about the bits in between. Even the sequence of events was somewhat hazy! As I read the stories in the Bible from beginning to end, it was the clarity that struck me; just how significant each section was to the next, and to the former. It was like seeing the whole and not just the segments, as can so often be the case.

So the aim of these books is basically that – to try and provide as full and complete a study as possible on specific characters. Looking at what is known of their life in sequence and drawing attention to the events that shaped them, one is able to follow the development of their relationship with, and understanding of God and the unfolding of his will and promises in their life.

Obviously with some stories spanning many books of the Bible not every detail can be included, but I hope that I have been as thorough as possible. Additionally, there may be some occasions when in order to keep the focus on the character in question, important events surrounding them may appear to be overlooked. This is in no way due to a lack of relevance of the events to their lives, but rather a lack of any detailed response or actions on their part during the events.

How to use these books

Each book is divided into eleven sections – ten character studies, with a review in the eleventh. Each section contains one lesson plan, three overhead sheets, one in-class worksheet and one take-home sheet. (I hope that there will be more than enough material for each session – far better to have to leave some out than be left short and have to make some up!)

Lesson plan

Before arriving at the lesson, make sure you've read the complete lesson plan! It may seem obvious but making sure you under-stand and agree with the contents will help you as you lead the meeting.

Each lesson plan begins with a Bible reading (or a Background Information section where necessary, to be read out first). All readings and verses throughout these books are taken from the NIV Bible, unless otherwise stated. The verses that correspond to the overhead pictures are listed in order so that the picture can be placed up when the verse is reached.

The main teaching on the reading is in the form of questions to be read out to the children and 'desired answers'. Make sure you have read the desired answers and lesson summaries and then, bearing those answers in mind, gently lead the discussion and the children's responses introducing the given answers along the way. (The answers are written in such a way that they can be read out if discussion proves difficult at times.)

Helpful points

- It is most important to encourage the children to think about and understand the story and the questions themselves. Do not step in with the 'answers' too quickly!

- Make sure that the children address each section before moving on – further explanation or re-reading may be necessary.

- Try and involve *all* the children. This may mean addressing the questions to specific individuals, or asking the children if they agree with any opinions offered, etc.

- Above all be encouraging! Make sure they know when they're right but don't feel silly if they're wrong.

- The additional material is there to be used where appropriate or practical. Worksheets are explained where necessary and puzzles that require answers in the take-home sheet are given.

- Each session ends with a prayer that can either be prayed by you or by one of the children.

Overheads

There are three overhead illustrations for each section. (If appropriate these can also be photocopied onto plain paper and used as colouring sheets.)

Worksheets

These are intended to be completed in lesson time, but most will work equally well as take-home sheets if necessary.

Take-home sheets

When answers are needed they are given in the lesson plan. Since the take-home sheets often contain questions relevant to the reading, I suggest that the sheets are brought back completed the following week and the answers given in class. This should encourage the children to complete the readings and questions as well as the puzzles.

I hope that these books prove helpful to you – please write to Kevin Mayhew Publishers with comments, ideas or suggestions that might be included in further work.

EPISODE 1

The Early Years

EPISODE 1

The Early Years

Background

God had always planned to send Jesus to man from the time Adam sinned. God made a promise to Abraham that salvation would come through his family – a family God would make into a nation special and protected for him because it was to be the nation into which Jesus would be born. Abraham's family grew and years later Joseph was born, who was eventually able to bring the entire family into Egypt and save them from famine. Hundreds of years after that the family – the Israelites – had become very numerous and filled the land. The Pharaoh of that day became afraid of their numbers so he turned them all into slaves to the Egyptians. Even this did not stop the Israelites growing, so Pharaoh ordered all baby Israelite boys to be drowned at birth.

Reading

Exodus 2:1-17.

Overheads

1 (v 6) Pharaoh's daughter sees baby Moses.
2 (v 12) Moses kills an Egyptian.
3 (v 17) Moses drives the shepherds away.

What this episode tells us

What we can learn from Moses
We must treat others as God treats us.

What we can learn about God
That he desires and blesses generosity in nature and deeds.

Discussion questions and desired answers

How was God good to Moses as a baby?
Pharaoh had ordered all Hebrew baby boys to be killed. Moses was hidden and put in the Nile in a basket and eventually saved by Pharaoh's daughter. Moses was therefore protected from Pharaoh.

Read Acts 7:22. How did this affect Moses?
He was given a safe and good upbringing and education.

Why did Moses, when he was older, kill the Egyptian slave master?
Because he was beating a Hebrew, one of Moses' own people.

Why did Moses rescue the women in the desert?
They were being mistreated by shepherds.

8

Can you see a connection in the way Moses acts as an adult to the way God acted towards him as a baby?

God protected and saved Moses as a baby. Here Moses is seen protecting and saving others.

What can we learn from this?

That we should treat people as God treats us.

Can you think of some examples we know God expects of us?

(John 13:34) Love each other as Jesus loves us.
(Col 3:13) Forgive as we are forgiven.
(Mat 18:33) Show mercy as it is shown to us.

Read Proverbs 11:24 and 25. How are these verses relevant?

They talk of giving and generosity. This does not just apply to material things like money and possessions but to time and to attitudes. Moses was generous in the way he wanted to give what God had given him. We too can recognise God's attitudes and blessings to us and be generous in the way we share those with others.

Additional material

Fun

'Whose Name Is It Anyway?' Group Game. Pharaoh's daughter named Moses saying it was because she 'drew him out of the water' (v 10). Moses is said to mean 'draw out'. Ask the children to either bring in the definitions of their names or, if you know the group, find them out during the week. Read out just the definitions and have the children write down who they think each belongs to. Add up the total correct for possible prizes at the end.

Further reading

Joseph is blessed and protected by God in Egypt where he prospers after his brothers left him for dead. Eventually Joseph is in a position to give to his father and even the brothers who betrayed him the prosperity and safety he has (Genesis 47:11-12).

Worksheet

Self-explanatory.

Take-home sheet

Egyptians left to right: Lonz, Plott, Obrovon, Raph, Wron. Victim: Plott.

Closing prayer

Dear God, thank you that you are such a good God. You are generous in your attitude and treatment of me as well as in your blessings and provision. Help me, Father, to recognise the generosity you show me so that I, in turn, can treat others in the same way. Amen.

Read Matthew 18:23-34. Draw in the missing characters, faces and bodies and fill in the speech bubbles to complete Jesus' parable, then answer the question below.

In what way is Jesus' parable relevant to the teaching today?

Moses killed an Egyptian slave master and it wasn't long before Pharaoh had found out! Using the clues below can you determine the identity of Moses' victim?

L R

Plott is closer to Raph than Lonz is.
Oorovon is not on an end.
Wron is not next to someone holding something or wearing a necklace.
Lonz and Plott are next to each other.
Oorovon has black hair.
Moses' victim was the second from the left.

His name is _____.

Moses in exile...

MOSES FLED FOR HIS LIFE WHEN PHARAOH LEARNT WHAT HAD HAPPENED. CAN YOU HELP HIM FIND A ROUTE THROUGH THE DESERT TO MIDIAN - MAKING SURE YOU PASS THROUGH THE WELL..!

MIDIAN

Read Exodus 2:23-25. When God looked down he saw the Egyptians mistreating the Israelites. Can you draw a ruler-straight line in this bird's-eye picture that joins all the dots together, does not cross itself but separates all the Egyptians on one side, and the Israelites on the other?

START

FINISH

EPISODE 2

The Burning Bush

The Burning Bush

Background

Moses married one of the women he rescued at the well and had a son by her. Moses was forty years old when he fled Egypt and for a further forty years lived with his wife and her family in Midian.

Reading

Exodus 3:1-7, 10-12, and 4:1-5, 10-17.

Overheads

1 (3:4) God calls to Moses from the burning bush.
2 (4:3) Moses' staff becomes a snake.
3 (4:13) Moses objects to God's commission.

What this episode tells us

What we can learn from Moses
That we should trust and believe God.

What we can learn about God
That his words and promises are true.

Discussion questions and desired answers

Look again at the things God says to Moses in today's reading. What assurances does God give Moses?
3:12. 'I will be with you . . . you will worship on this mountain.'
4:5. A sign others will believe.
4:12. 'I will help you speak and teach you what to say.'
4:15. 'I will help both of you speak and teach you what to do.'

Why does God become angry with Moses in 4:14?
In spite of God's assurances Moses doesn't believe he can do it and doesn't want to. Effectively he is not trusting God.

Encourage the children to imagine they are Moses. Describe the scene: The Bush – the voice of God himself actually talking to you! Do you think you would argue or disbelieve something God actually spoke and promised directly to you?
We would probably like to imagine we wouldn't! (Encourage personal response here, too.)

Do you think you believe what God promises?
Allow a response.

We might not literally <u>hear</u> God speak directly to us like Moses did, but there are many many things God assures and promises us in the Bible, his Living Word. Can you think of some?

John 3:16. God's love for us and eternal life.
2 Corinthians 5:17. A new life in Christ.
Matthew 6:14. Forgiveness.
Matthew 28:20. Jesus' continuing presence.
These are just some of the promises. Encourage the children to think of as many as they can. Alternatively before the 'answer' is given children could be given time to write down as many of God's promises as they can think of. Take time to read their answers out.

Do we always believe God?

Unfortunately not! Sometimes it may be easy for us to believe some things God says – for example, that we will go to heaven – but we may not truly believe he loves us or values us.

How do we know we can believe God?

Because the Bible shows that he keeps his word. (Read 1 Kings 8:56, Psalms 119:160, John 17:17.)

Additional material

Lesson aid

Depending on how you led the discussions, a personal list of promises for the children to keep may prove beneficial. Perhaps even written as a bookmark or poster?

Fun

'God's true, but are we?' Group Game. Have the children write down a brief story of something that actually happened, or sounds like it might have happened to them! Children could either read out their own stories or the teacher could read them out. The other children must vote true or false. Keep score if desired. (Statements of facts could be used instead of stories if preferred.)

Worksheet

Self-explanatory.

Take-home sheet

Code: 'I do not know the Lord, and I will not let Israel go.' (Exodus 5:2.)
Material piece: D.

Closing prayer

Dear Lord, you promise and assure me personally of so many things throughout your work and they are all true. Help me to really believe not just some but all of your words, deep in my heart. I thank you that you are faithful. Amen.

Copy the correct squares into the appropriate places to complete the picture of Moses and the burning bush.
When you have finished read Exodus 3:13-15 and complete Moses' and God's speech bubbles in your own words.
(Cutting and pasting may be used as an alternative to drawing.)

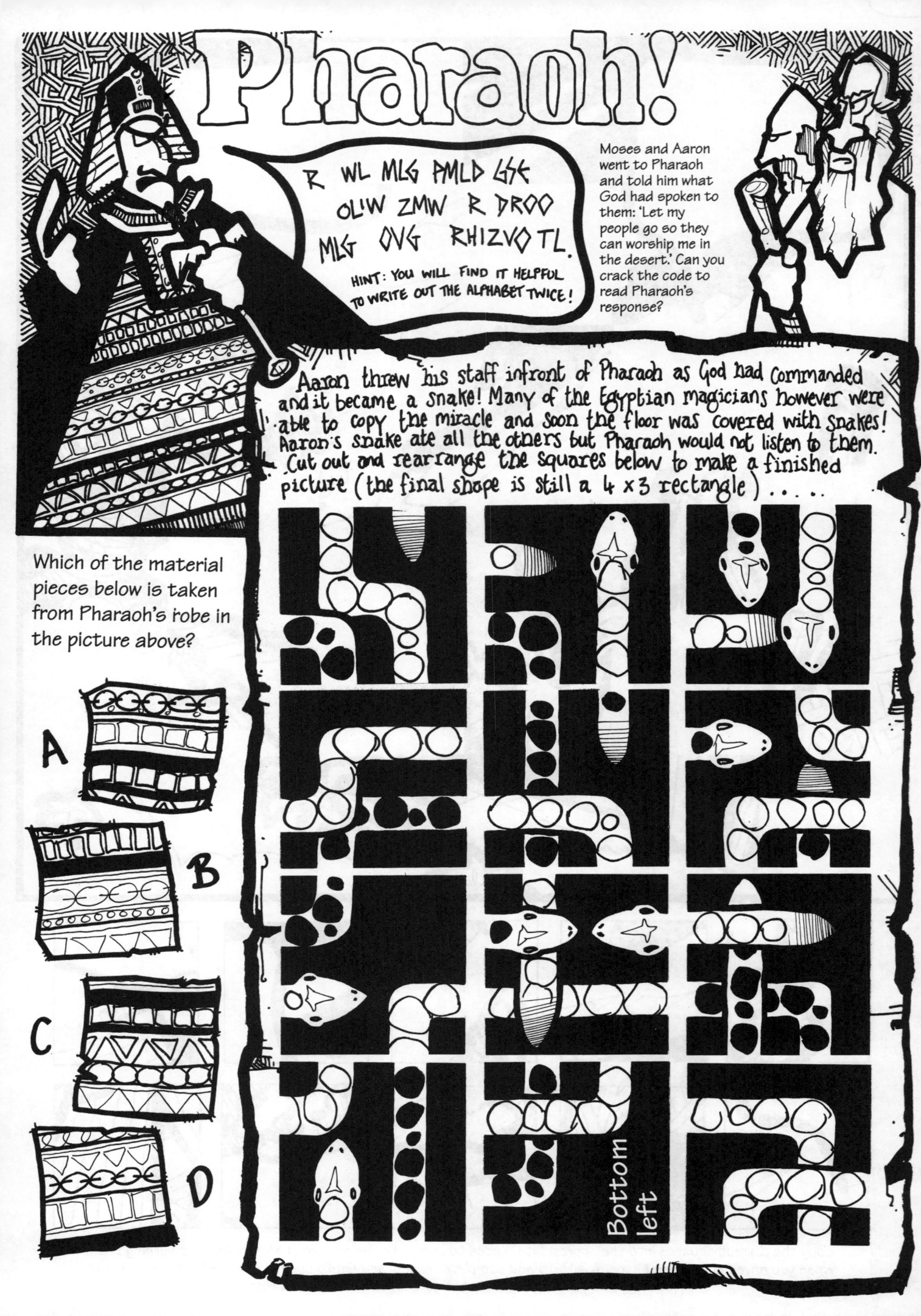

Pharaoh!

R WL MLG PMLD GSE OL!W ZMW R DROO MLG OVG RHIZVO TL.

HINT: YOU WILL FIND IT HELPFUL TO WRITE OUT THE ALPHABET TWICE!

Moses and Aaron went to Pharaoh and told him what God had spoken to them: 'Let my people go so they can worship me in the desert.' Can you crack the code to read Pharaoh's response?

Aaron threw his staff infront of Pharaoh as God had commanded and it became a snake! Many of the Egyptian magicians however were able to copy the miracle and soon the floor was covered with snakes! Aaron's snake ate all the others but Pharaoh would not listen to them. Cut out and rearrange the squares below to make a finished picture (the final shape is still a 4 x 3 rectangle) . . . . .

Which of the material pieces below is taken from Pharaoh's robe in the picture above?

A

B

C

D

Bottom left

EPISODE 3

The Plagues

EPISODE 3

The Plagues

Background

Moses and Aaron went to Pharaoh on the banks of the Nile. As God commanded, Aaron struck the water with his staff and it turned to blood, so Pharaoh might believe in God. All the water in Egypt became blood but Pharaoh would not free the Israelites. God caused a plague of frogs to cover the land yet still Pharaoh chose not to believe.

Reading

Exodus 8:16-30.

Overheads

1 (background) The Nile turns to blood.
2 (v 17) Aaron strikes the dust.
3 (v 25) Pharaoh summons Moses among the flies.

What this episode tells us

What we can learn from Moses
We should not compromise but be consistent and obedient.

What we can learn about God
That his ways are true.

Discussion questions and desired answers

Read Exodus 7:16. What does God want?
His people to be freed to worship him in the desert.

What does Pharaoh say in Exodus 8:25?
They may worship in the land (Egypt).

What is Pharaoh doing?
Offering a compromise.

How does Moses respond to this?
He does not accept.

This is the first of three attempted compromises by Pharaoh (see Exodus 10:11 and 24 for the other two if necessary). Moses rejects all of them. What does this tell us about Moses?
He is not willing to compromise God's will. In order not to compromise it is first essential to know what God's will is. Moses listened to God and knew – therefore he wouldn't settle for second best – only God's best.

If Moses represents us as Christians doing God's will, what does Pharaoh represent?
The temptation to compromise with evil. In verse 25 Pharaoh says, 'Worship God, but here in Egypt' – effectively: 'Be a Christian but still be a slave to sin.' Compromise is not always a bad thing – e.g. to resolve family arguments, political disagreements, church differences, etc. It is only compromise with evil which is bad.

What does Paul say in Romans 12:2?
We should not conform to the ways of the world. (If you feel it is relevant discuss ways of conforming that the children may be experiencing, i.e. peer pressure, sex, drugs. Even if these are still to come, it is good to make a decision now.)

After each plague Pharaoh said he would free the Israelites then changed his mind. Do you know how many plagues there were?
Ten.

Moses went through the same procedure ten times. What does this tell us about him?
As well as not compromising he was consistently faithful and obedient.

How is this relevant to not compromising?
Like Moses we need to be consistent and faithful to God's will. Not to conform is not just a one-off decision but an on-going attitude and desire to do and seek after God's best – whatever the circumstances.

How can we trust God's way?
We saw last week how God is true – his words and his promises are to be believed. If God is true then we know his ways are also true, to be trusted and worth not compromising. (Revelation 15:3, 'Just and true are your ways, king of the ages'.)

Additional material

Fun

'Boils' Group Game. The sixth plague was a plague of boils. All the children are Egyptians except one – and guess what they are! That child is a boil and needs to catch other Egyptians to spread the plague. Each tagged or caught Egyptian is now a boil after the rest. The winner is the last boil-free Egyptian. Lovely!

Further reading

Daniel 3:8-28. Shadrach, Meshach and Abednego refuse to compromise and worship an idol. God protects them.
Daniel 6:10-24. Daniel's refusal to compromise. God again protects.
Acts 5:17-32. The apostles continue in their preaching in spite of persecution.
1 Samuel 24. David spares Saul, choosing God's way and not the ways of his men.

Worksheet

Self-explanatory.

Take-home sheet

'God is in control.'

Closing prayer

Dear Father God, thank you that I know not only your words but your ways to be true. Help me, Lord, to recognise your way in every situation so that I may follow it. Please help me when this is hard – I trust you, Lord. Amen.

```
P K E X Z S L F U H   S J Y B K D B P
B M O F N G S Q P A   H Q T X L U N Z
L G D R Y R H K N I   L E Z E G O A U
V A J O H T X U X L   K I R A C T E O
Q H U G A Y I E T S   G K D W V M Z V
F W B S N J W C O T   C F P H T A E P
E C T C I A D D O O   L B C F P H Y T
G G I K N Z T M T R   B L U I F S K N
Y R M D Q B V S W M   M C G H Q X M S
P E S L J N E E Y A   E N S V I R J Y
T F O R P V A I V Z   O D J W W L W Q
Z E T P I Y G L A J   Z O Y A A X R V
B U D L M H U F V Q   N N J T V R L F
A H L J O X I Q B R   P K B E F W M U
A S W O Z C F P O A   B N O R X B K S
F C K C N J U B P I   M M I D M Y G A
V R X I L A T S W C   Q L L E E C Y H
D B L Y Q S K O T H   D R S U G Z E T
G Q D A R K N E S S   H Q E G W N J R
I H M I R E R L U G   L S R A A X D I
P G F S V B M X D E   T S W L O J Q N
E N T K W S N Z Y D   F U T P H M Z S
J F O U D C T E K G   V U K I B P C L
```

From Exodus 7 to chapter 11, God sends ten plagues against Egypt. Can you fill in the missing words for the title of each plague and find them in the wordsearch?

1. _____ of the _____ changed into _____.

2. _____ cover the land.

3. _____ becomes _____.

4. _____ of _____.

5. _____ die.

6. Festering _____ will break out.

7. _____ on men and animals.

8. _____ of _____.

9. _____ over _____

10. _____ of every _____.

(All words from NIV.)

THE PASSOVER

The final plague was to be the death of every firstborn – man or animal. God instructed the Israelites to put the blood of a sacrificed lamb on their doorposts and the angel of death would see the blood and pass that house by. In the picture below, each black door-lintel represents the blood. Can you draw a line that does not cross itself but makes a route to join up every house without the blood on the door. You can draw up, down, left, right or diagonally.

START

FINISH

The Passover marked the end of Israelite slavery and is still a very significant time in the Jewish calendar celebrated and remembered every year.

EVERY EGYPTIAN FIRSTBORN CHILD DIED AND PHARAOH GAVE IN AT LAST. THE EGYPTIANS WERE NOW SCARED OF GOD AND GAVE THE ISRAELITES GOLD, SILVER AND CLOTHES TO LEAVE AS SOON AS POSSIBLE! THAT DAY OVER A MILLION ISRAELITES LEFT EGYPT!

WHAT DO ALL THE PLAGUES AGAINST EGYPT TELL US....

(take the first letter of each thing above and rearrange them below to answer the above question)

Read Exodus 12:3, 7 and 13. What saved the Israelites?

Read John 1:29. What does John call Jesus?

Can you see a parallel between the Passover and us as Christians?

EPISODE 4

Through the Red Sea

EPISODE 4

Through the Red Sea

Background

(The children should have learnt about the Passover from the last episode's take-home sheet, though it might be worth a recap if necessary.) Moses led over a million Israelites out of Egypt after the Passover. They went into the desert with God guiding them as a pillar of cloud by day and a pillar of fire by night. Almost as soon as they'd left, however, Pharaoh regretted his decision and set out in pursuit of Israel . . .

Reading

Exodus 14:9-16, 21-31.

Overheads

1 (v 13) Moses urges the people to trust God.
2 (v 22) Crossing the Red Sea.
3 (v 28) The Egyptians are drowned.

What this episode tells us

What we can learn from Moses
That we must trust in God, whatever the circumstances.

What we can learn about God
That he is always in control and will not forsake us.

Discussion questions and desired answers

What did we learn from this episode?
God's ways are true and we, like Moses, should be consistent and faithful in following them, not compromising along the way.

Moses had obeyed God and eventually Pharaoh released the Israelites. But what happened at the beginning of today's reading?
Pharaoh has changed his mind and is pursuing the Israelites.

The Israelites have been following God as he guided them in a pillar of cloud or fire. Where are they now?
By the shores of the Red Sea, with Pharaoh's army behind them, literally trapped.

What happens in verses 11 and 12?
The Israelites, recognising they are trapped, are afraid and panic.

How does Moses respond? (verses 13 and 14)
Moses assures them not to worry because God will deliver them.

32

Trapped between the sea and the army, Moses seems amazingly confident! How do you think he can be?

Moses knows it was his obedience to God which we saw in the last episode that has led them to this point. Moses trusts that God's ways are best and God is in control. If God's way has led them there then God must know why, even if Moses doesn't!

How do you think Moses' situation can be relevant to us?

Sometimes following God's ways, living as we know he would want us to and not compromising can put us in seemingly difficult situations, yet when we are faithful to God we can be sure he will be faithful to us. If difficulties arise because of our being true to God we can trust those to him, just as Moses does here.

God opens up the sea as an escape for the Israelites. What can we learn from this?

A number of things. Firstly God is always in control! Secondly he doesn't always act when we think he should. It wasn't until the Israelites were trapped that God acted and it was in a manner most unexpected! Lastly God's ways are here proven to be the best; not only did the Israelites escape but the Egyptians were all drowned, rendering the Israelites completely safe. God is definitely worth trusting!

Additional material

Further reading

1 Samuel 29:1-11. David is forced to join his enemies to escape Saul, whom God has shown him he should not kill. Now the Philistines, with David, are marching against Saul. David is seemingly about to be compromised when an argument between the Philistines allows him to escape the battle and not have his loyalties discovered. God steps in to protect him at the last moment.

Prayer time

The Israelites had cried out to God to save them when they were slaves in Egypt. God answered their prayer. If relevant spend some time either sharing prayer answers or thanking God for answers to prayer. Additionally, pray for children that have prayer requests or have not yet seen answers for what they are praying.

Worksheet

'In your unfailing love you will lead the people you have redeemed. In your strength you will guide them.' (Exodus 15:13.)

Take-home sheet

Word – 'Manna'.

Closing prayer

Thank you, Father God, that you are always in control. Help me always to remember this and to trust you always. Thank you that you always care for me and always know exactly the situation I am in. I trust my life to you because your ways are the best. Amen.

When the waters of the Red Sea closed in again and drowned the Egyptians, Israel was truly safe. The people praised God and an Israelite named Miriam led the women in song and dance with her tambourine. Can you work out some of the song they sang?

GOD'S PROVISION

AFTER 3 DAYS IN THE DESERT THE ISRAELITES GREW VERY THIRSTY BUT THE FIRST WATER THEY CAME TO WAS TOO BITTER TO DRINK AND THEY BEGAN TO COMPLAIN CAN YOU SPOT 10 DIFFERENCES IN THE WATER'S REFLECTION IN THE PICTURE BELOW?

The Israelites soon began to complain because they were hungry. God provided a special food for them. Colour in each shape with a dot to reveal the name of this food.

This food appeared on the ground in the mornings, like dew. It came from heaven and looked like frost.

God also caused quails to be blown into the camp. Can you find two sets of identical quails below?

Can you write or draw here something God has provided or blessed you with?

EPISODE 5

The Giving of the Law

EPISODE 5

The Giving of the Law

Background

God led the Israelites through the desert until they reached Mount Sinai a few months later. There they set up camp.

Reading

Exodus 19:3-12, 16-19, and 20:18-24.

Overheads

1 (19:7) Moses speaks to the elders.
2 (19:18) God descends on Mount Sinai.
3 (20:21) Moses enters the thick darkness.

What this episode tells us

It is necessary in this episode to focus on the law and grace through which we now live. Consequently there isn't any direct teaching on Moses. It may also be necessary to read out several discussion answers as it is more unlikely that children will have answers of their own.

Discussion questions and desired answers

What has happened to Israel so far?
God has brought them out of Egypt where they were slaves and is leading them across the desert.

Had the Israelites done anything to deserve this?
No. God chose to save them by Grace.

What is Grace?
Grace is something freely given that is not necessarily deserved. In this case, Israel's redemption.

Read verses 5 and 6. What is God's promise to Israel?
If they obey him, he will bless them and lead them to a Promised Land.

In verse 8 the people accept God's promise. God comes down to Mount Sinai and gives Moses the law. This includes the Ten Commandments. Can you remember them? (Use Exodus 20 to help if necessary.) The Ten Commandments are the most well known part of the law. The entire law detailed exact directions for Israel to live by. What was the purpose of the law?
The law showed the standard it was necessary to achieve in order to have relationship with God. God is so holy and so perfect that only meeting the exact requirements of the law would make us acceptable to him.

Can we do it?
No we can't. It would mean never sinning; that is how exact the requirements are. That is another reason for the law; to show us that it is impossible to meet God's standards through anything we do.

One Person did meet the exact requirements of the law. Who?
Jesus.

If that is true, why did Jesus die?

Part of the law required sacrifices to 'atone' for sin. The blood of animal sacrifices did not remove sin but allowed the sinner a 'pardon' and another chance. Having lived to the law's exact requirements Jesus was a perfect atoning sacrifice able not only to pardon sin but remove it altogether. When we believe in Jesus we accept that he was a perfect sacrifice that removes our sin.

Why can we have relationship with God as Christians?

Jesus lives inside us as Christians. When God looks on us he sees Jesus – the perfect atoning sacrifice – and because of Jesus' perfection in us, God is able to have relationship with us because our sin, through Jesus, is removed.

Do we deserve this?

No, because we are sinners and should have to live out the law to meet God, but it is grace freely given to us that provides such privilege.

Can you see the difference between law and grace?

Law made it up to man to become good enough for God. Grace, which we live by since Jesus, makes it all because of Jesus. It's nothing we do or deserve. That's why Jesus is so essential to Christianity. It is only through Jesus that we are able to be saved from sin and know God.

Additional material

Fun

'Watch that Mountain!' Group Game. As soon as the people had accepted God's proposed law, God put a boundary between himself and the people. No one but Moses could touch the mountain. In a safe space mark out a 'boundary' that can be walked around (a circle or square in the middle of the room). Children, blindfolded, must move around the outside without crossing the boundary. Additionally you could gradually expand the boundary or include obstacles (chairs, etc.) Tell the children as you do it and they'll have to navigate by memory. Anyone who touches the 'mountain' then stands in the middle without a blindfold and watches the others, perhaps grabbing or pulling them in if they touch or cross it. The winner could be the last person still navigating the boundary. (It may be wise to disallow walking around the outskirts of the room against the walls as that's a touch too easy, unless they're out for touching those too?!)

Worksheet

Self-explanatory.

Take-home sheet

Squares A, D, G and I.

Closing prayer

Dear Lord Jesus, thank you so much that through your death you have given me the right to become a child of God. Thank you that you live in me and have taken away my sin. Please lead me and help me live in a way that shows my thankfulness both to you and to others. Amen.

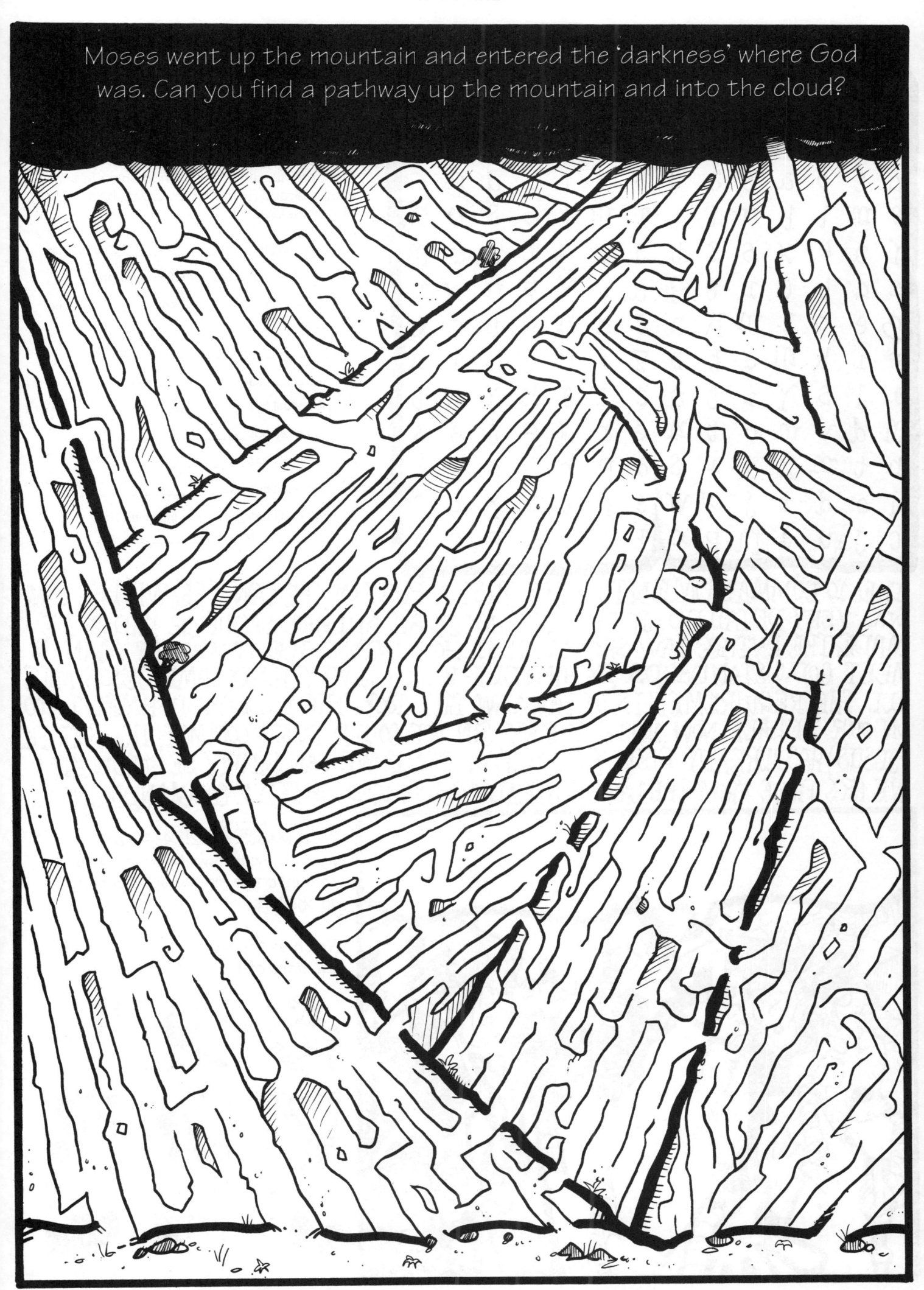

Moses went up the mountain and entered the 'darkness' where God was. Can you find a pathway up the mountain and into the cloud?

THE LAW

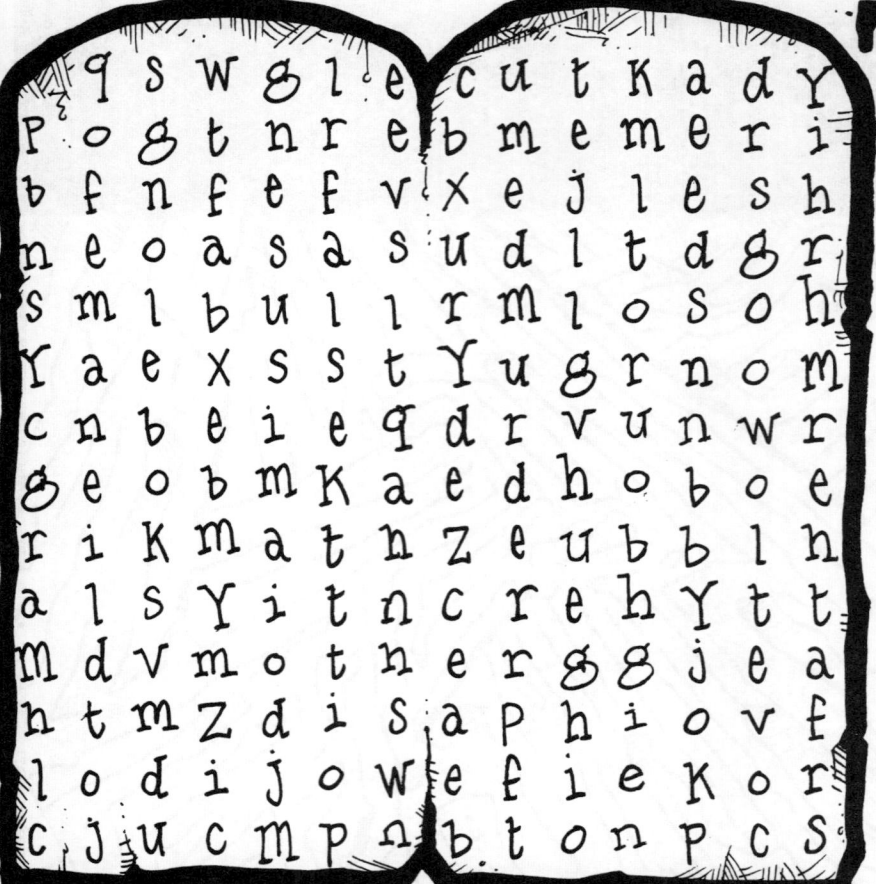

Can you fill in the missing words from the Ten Commandments and find them in the wordsearch? (Use Exodus 20 to help you. NIV translation.)

1. You shall have no _____ _____ before me.
2. You shall not make for yourselves an _____.
3. You shall not _____ the _____ of the Lord.
4. _____ the _____ day.
5. _____ your _____ and _____.
6. You shall not _____.
7. You shall not _____ _____.
8. You shall not _____.
9. You shall not give _____ _____.
10. You shall not _____ anything that _____ to your _____.

THE 10 COMMANDMENTS WERE JUST A PART OF THE LAW. THE WHOLE LAW WAS VERY DETAILED- IF PEOPLE SINNED AN ANIMAL SACRIFICE HAD TO BE MADE. THE ENTIRE LAW SHOWED JUST HOW IMPOSSIBLE IT WAS FOR MAN TO MEET GOD'S STANDARDS BY HIMSELF- WHICH IS WHY JESUS CAME. JESUS MET ALL THE REQUIREMENTS OF THE LAW BUT TOOK THE FULL PUNISHMENT TOO, ON OUR BEHALF. NOW WITH EVERY SIN WE COULD EVER COMMIT, THE SACRIFICE (JESUS) HAS ALREADY DIED. BECAUSE OF JESUS WE CAN SIMPLY BE FORGIVEN! WE ARE FREE FROM THE LAW- INSTEAD JESUS HIGHLIGHTED 2 COMMANDMENTS...

Read Matthew 22:34-40 and in your own words write what Jesus said into the empty speech bubble on the left.

Which of the following squares are not part of the picture on the left?

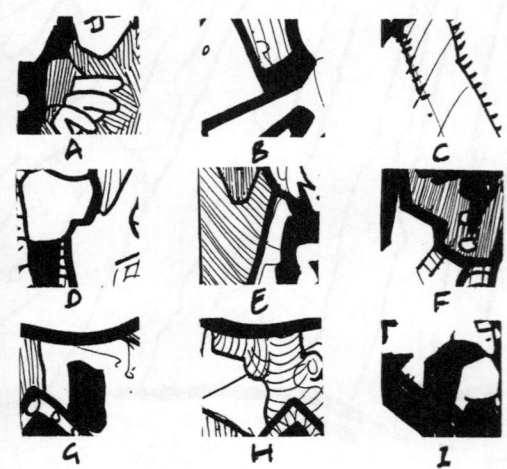

EPISODE 6

The Golden Calf

EPISODE 6

The Golden Calf

Reading

Exodus 32:1-4, 7-20.

Overheads

1 (v 4) The golden calf.
2 (v 11) Moses seeks God's favour.
3 (v 19) Moses approaches the camp.

What this episode tells us

What we can learn from Moses
We should control our anger and not let it rule our response.

What we can learn about God
That he is merciful.

Discussion questions and desired answers

What have the Israelites done wrong in today's episode?
Against God's explicit commandments they have made another idol to worship.

How does Moses find out about this?
God tells him.

Is Moses angered?
Yes! He even smashed the stone tablets because he was so angry.

Was anger Moses' first response?
No. His first response was to plead for God to have mercy on the Israelites.

What does this tell us about Moses?
Although he clearly recognised the extent of the Israelites' sin he didn't let his anger determine his initial response, but took time to seek God first.

What are your first thoughts when you are angered?
Usually they are of retaliation or vindication (proving yourself right).

Why then do you think it might be harmful to act on these emotions?
They are not constructive or right. If our first response is retaliation or vindication we need to wait and act on a more constructive emotion.

Moses spent time with God before going to the Israelites. His anger was still severe, so what do you suppose was the benefit of his prayers?

Not acting in anger allows us to focus better. We are able to be angry at the sin – the action – but not the sinner. The sin of the Israelites was severe as was Moses' response to it, but his response was not hatred towards them.

What could we learn from this?

Not to act out of anger. The way we do this can vary and each of us needs to be aware of how best to take our focus of anger off the person themselves and on to the situation or the deed, etc. This might mean praying first, or being alone, even counting to ten before responding! Proverbs 14:17 says, 'A quick-tempered man does foolish things.' Anger can be destructive and we must learn to control it, not let it control us. As we saw in Episode 1, we should treat others as God treats us. Is God quick to anger with us?

Additional material

Further reading

Mark 11:15-17. Jesus drives out the traders from the temple, showing anger at their sin as opposed to them as people. (All four gospel accounts record Jesus overturning tables and scattering money and livestock but never striking the actual traders.)

Fun

'Musical Israelites' Group Game. When Moses came into the Israelites' camp they were singing and dancing. Select one person to be Moses who leaves the room whilst the others sing and dance. Moses may burst in at any time whereupon everyone must freeze until he has left. Any Israelite Moses spies moving is out, and so on and so on!

Worksheet

Self-explanatory. You will need scissors and Pritt stick or Sellotape for this.

Take-home sheet

f, b, d, i, h.
Sequence: 1, 10, 5, 9, 7, 3, 8, 4, 6, 2.

Closing prayer

Dear Jesus, thank you for your life in me. I pray that your actions and attitudes become more and more a part of mine so that I can respond to others as I know you would to me. Help me, Lord, to be slow to anger and quick to forgive. Amen.

Cut out each of the squares on the right and fold each piece diagonally in half where you can see the separate image. Stick these down and see if you can arrange the pieces to find the commandment God gave the Israelites.

When you have found it, stick your picture together with Sellotape and turn it over. Unfortunately, that's how the Israelites responded!

Although we might think we would never be as foolish as to worship an idol we must not forget that an idol isn't just a statue or image. It can be anything we value more highly than God. Hobbies, music, money, fashion, friends can all become idols to us if we're not careful.

PUNISHMENTS

GOD INSCRIBED THE LAW ONTO 2 STONE TABLETS WHICH MOSES SMASHED WHEN HE SAW THE ISRAELITES' IDOL....

CAN YOU MATCH THE MISSING STONE PIECES

MOSES MELTED THE CALF ON THE FIRE AND SCATTERED THE GOLD ON THE WATER THE ISRAELITES HAD TO DRINK! CAN YOU FIND A WAY THROUGH THE GOLD?!

Moses asked the Israelites who were willing to follow God. Only the tribe of Levi responded. As a punishment for this and for the idol, the tribe of Levi was ordered to walk through the camp killing the unbelievers. That day 3,000 Israelites died. Can you join all the numbers together in a ruler-straight line that passes through each of the people, representing 100 Israelites each. Write the sequence here:

start _____

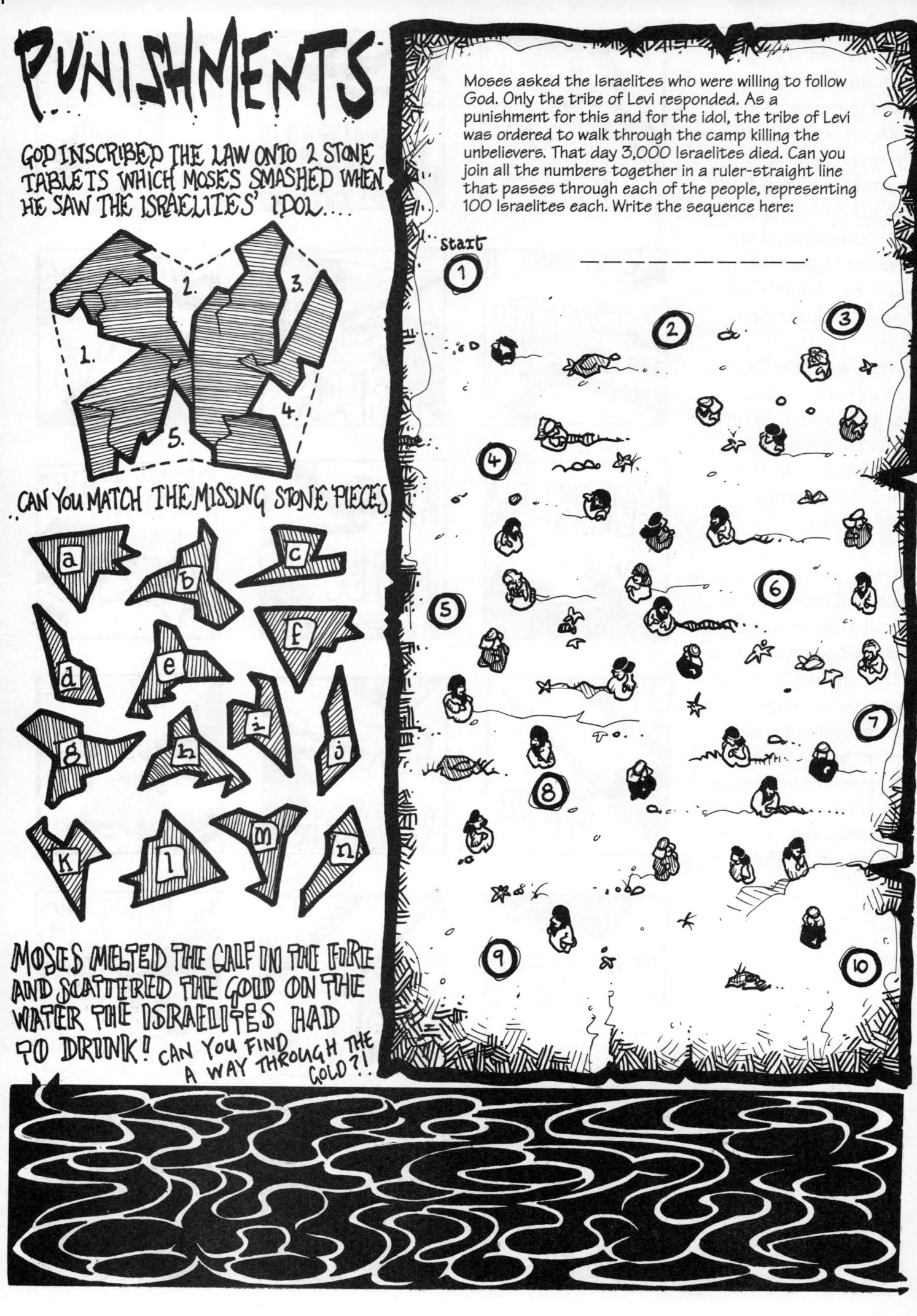

EPISODE 7

God's Glory

EPISODE 7

God's Glory

Background

After their sin with the golden calf, God commands Israel to resume their journey to the Promised Land but says his presence will no longer go before them as it had done.

Reading

Exodus 33:7-14, 18-23 and 34:5-8.

Overheads

1 (33:9) The pillar of cloud at the Tent of Meeting.
2 (33:13) Moses' prayer to God.
3 (34:6) God's glory passes by Moses.

What this episode tells us

What we can learn from Moses
To have a continuing desire for more of God.

What we can learn about God
That he blesses such desire and gives of himself to us.

Discussion questions and desired answers

In what ways so far has Moses actually seen God?
On Mount Sinai, as a pillar of cloud and fire, in the burning bush, face to face in the Tent of Meeting.

How would you describe Moses' relationship with God?
Awesome, unique, amazing, close, special, etc.

What does Moses ask God in verse 18?
He asks God to show his glory.

Considering all Moses has seen and experienced of God is it greedy or ungrateful to ask for even more?
No it is not.

Why not?
God desires a relationship with us. There should never be a point where a relationship can't get any better or grow any deeper. Psalm 105:4 says 'seek his face always'.

How can we tell from this passage that God is pleased with Moses' request?
He does what Moses' asks – he shows Moses his glory.

How should we be like Moses in today's episode?

We can always be grateful and thankful for God speaking to us, showing us things, for where our relationship currently stands, but we should never become satisfied so that we do not desire it to get any better. And also, like Moses, we can ask of God and expect him to draw closer. If we've heard God speak or had God touch us in some way we will ask him to do so again. If we've never had God speak to us or touch us, we should ask him to. Psalm 34:8 says, 'taste and see that the Lord is good.' God expects and wants us to taste and see – and when we find it's good shouldn't we want to do it again . . . and again?

Additional material

Lesson aid

Example – if relevant, question someone about a close friendship they have. How did it form (by spending time with each other, beginning to know each other's likes and dislikes, etc.) Draw the comparison to God and a deepening relationship. Friends *want* to spend time together, lovers have to, etc.

Practical and fun! – Bring perhaps a large bar of chocolate or bag of sweets and give a piece to each child at the beginning of the discussion. Place the rest in a very prominent and accessible place but don't offer any more. If at any point someone asks to have another or moves to take another, first ask why and then let them. Continue to not offer but allow anyone who asks or takes to have as much as they like (in the event all the children fail to ask or take, you may have to drop hints to encourage. For example: 'Well I suppose I'll take these home although I don't know who'll eat it – none of us likes chocolate!') Hopefully the children's reasons for wanting more will be because they tasted it and like it. Once the bar or packet is eaten you can draw the relevant comparison to God: 'taste and see, etc.' When you see and agree you want more, God's there to let you have more!

Worksheet

Self-explanatory.

Take-home sheet

From left to right: bread, plate, oil, candlestick, cup.

Closing prayer

Dear Father God. It's so amazing to know that I can actually have a relationship with you and you really want me to! Please reveal to me more of yourself. I truly want to know you more and love you deeper. Thank you, Jesus. Amen.

BUILDING THE TABERNACLE

God gave Moses instructions to build a special tent that would protect the tablets of law and be a place where offerings could be made. The very innermost room was to be called the Holy of Holies and it would be from there that God would now speak to Moses. The Israelites shared all the gold, silver and good materials they had and they made and built the tabernacle just as God had directed.

Study the picture above for two minutes then cover it and see if you can answer the following questions – but don't read the questions first!

1. How many birds were there in the sky?
2. What was the man on the ladder carrying?
3. How many candles could fit on the candlestick?
4. What colour hair did the man with the hammer have?
5. How many women were there sewing?
6. How many blocks were there around the fire?
7. Did the man hammering have a bracelet on?
8. How many objects were there on the candlestick maker's work surface?
9. How many people were there in the picture?
10. Was the candlestick maker bare-chested or wearing a top?

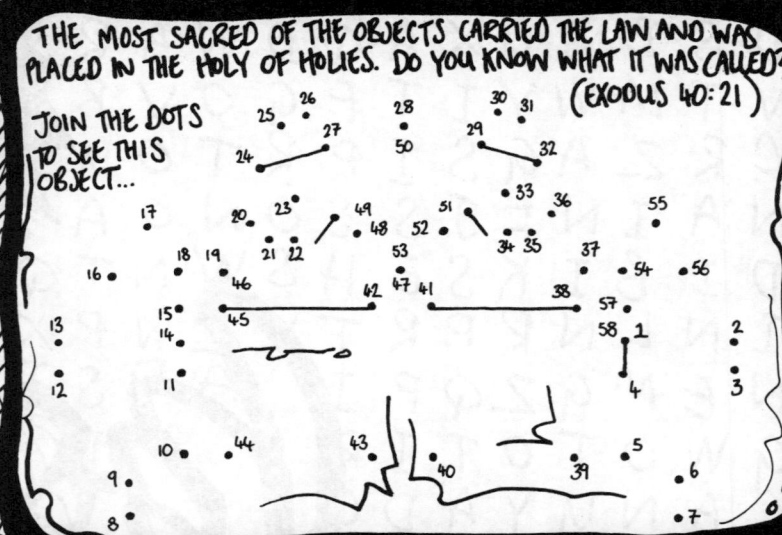

THE MOST SACRED OF THE OBJECTS CARRIED THE LAW AND WAS PLACED IN THE HOLY OF HOLIES. DO YOU KNOW WHAT IT WAS CALLED? (EXODUS 40:21)

JOIN THE DOTS TO SEE THIS OBJECT...

READ EXODUS 40:33-38
WHAT HAPPENED WHEN THE TABERNACLE WAS FINISHED?

HOW DID THE ISRAELITES KNOW WHEN TO TRAVEL?

The outer room contained a golden table and an altar. From the clues below can you draw or write the objects on the left onto the table below in their correct order?

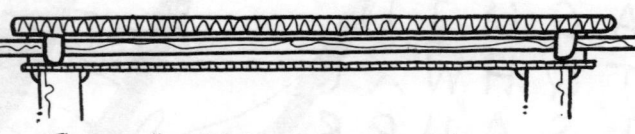

The candlestick is not on an end, but is closer to one than the oil is.
The cup is to the right of the oil.
The bread is closer to the plate than it is to the candlestick.
The bread is not next to the oil.

EPISODE 8

Complaints and Hardship

EPISODE 8   Complaints and Hardship

Background

With the Tabernacle completed the Israelites continued their journey to the Promised Land. Wherever they set up camp the tabernacle was the first thing to be erected. Moses would speak to God before the Ark of the Covenant in the Holy of Holies.

Reading

Numbers 11:4-6, 10-20, 31-34.

Overheads

1 (v 5) The Israelites complain.
2 (v 13) Moses pleads with God.
3 (v 31) Quail are blown in from the sea.

What this episode tells us

What we can learn from Moses
We should have total honesty with God.

What we can learn about God
That he is there for us in the hard times and sees our heart's attitude.

Discussion questions and desired answers

What are the Israelites complaining against in verses 4 and 5?
Their lack of meat to eat: too much manna!

What was manna?
Most importantly it was God's specific (and requested: Exodus 16:3-4) provision to them.

What else do the Israelites say? (verse 20)
'Why did we ever leave Egypt?'

What does this show us?
Not only are they ungrateful for God's provision but also for his entire plan and method of redemption to them as a nation. They look with favour back at their captivity rather than with faith towards God's promise.

What is God's response to their attitude?
God is angered and eventually punishes them through a plague (verse 33).

Moses also complains to God in this episode. What is his complaint?
He cannot cope with the Israelites; it has become too much to bear. As a reluctant leader in the first place (Exodus 4:13) he can no longer cope with the people constantly looking to him and not to God (verse 13).

What is God's response to Moses?
He answers Moses' plea and provides help for him.

What does the difference in God's response to both complaints tell us?
The nature of the complaints was different. The Israelites angered God but Moses received God's favour.

What do you think was different about the two complaints?
Their motive and attitude of heart. The Israelites were ungrateful and untrusting. They were consistently selfish and refused to acknowledge God's sovereignty. Moses had been faithful to God and still intended to be, yet the extent of their complaining finally wore him into the ground and he poured out his heart to God.

What can we learn from Moses?
It is OK to be honest with God. Moses felt he could no longer cope. He felt completely lost. He even wished God had never called him to lead the Israelites! Yet God cannot be shocked or surprised! He sees our hearts and knows how we have tried, how we have responded to difficulties and he wants us to tell him how we feel; to be honest and let him share our burdens (Psalm 68:19). God wants our whole lives to be open and shared with him and if that means he sees us or hears us when we feel at our worst then he wants that too, especially since he is the only one who can truly help!

Additional material

Further reading

Can we talk, Lord? by David Gatward (Kevin Mayhew Publishers, 1992). A best-selling collection of real and honest prayers from a teenager's heart, written in the language of youth.

Fun

'Greedy Israelites' Game. (A variation on a popular party piece!) You will need a big bag of marshmallows to represent quails! (Somewhat different in appearance to the genuine article but undoubtedly more suitable!) The object is to see who can get the most marshmallows into their mouth and still be able to repeat the phrase, 'Mmmmm! Lovely Meat!' between each one. This can be done individually or with two children ('Israelites') facing each other. It is best to have a towel to wear and a spitting-out bucket to hand. Perhaps partners could feed their players quails one at a time. Have fun!

Worksheet

Psalm 55:22. 'Cast your cares on the Lord and he will sustain you.'

Take-home sheet

Shaphat: D3. Igal: K5. Palti: F5. Gaddi: B1. Sethur: I6. Geuel: G4. Joshua: F1. Shammua: I1. Caleb: B5. Gaddiel: I3. Ammiel: F4. Nahbi: G6.

Closing prayer

Dear Lord Jesus, thank you so much that I can always turn to you. In happiness or in sadness I know that you always want to listen and can always help me. Thank you that I know I can trust you, Jesus. Amen.

① VTPHEBROILDROSARCKTRSDEPE
ECQASWSTPYONUIRMCARIPELS

CLUE: UNDER THE OLD OAK TREE

② clue: unite the farthest parts...

ovtadmlnabrvwqgsilmcenvrazypldfnclrestioumevln

③ TIRENLTRCEOTRESHALDET

clue: whatever's left when you've taken certain letters away
(and done a spot of rearranging!)

④ sagimfwrsaoneendwiaufnpddarhifel

CLUE: BEGIN AT ONE END AND USE EVERY THIRD AFTER IT...

⑤ clue: if the first becomes the last ...and so on...

DROOHFHGZRMBLF

⑥ mjprlbhiKpscldsegtafnqacm✓

Clue: where there are two, take one

ANSWER:

① _ _ _ _ _ _ _ _ _ _ _ _ _ _ ② _ _ ③ _ _ _

_ _ _ _ ④ _ _ _ _ _ _ ⑤ _ _ _ _ _ _

_ _ _ ⑥ _ _ _ _ 55:22

Spies exploring Canaan

The Israelites soon arrived at the Promised Land. Moses selected one person from each tribe to go and explore the land and report back to them after forty days. From the clues below can you work out where on the map each of the spies is and write the grid reference for their location in the boxes under their names? (No two spies are on the same square.)

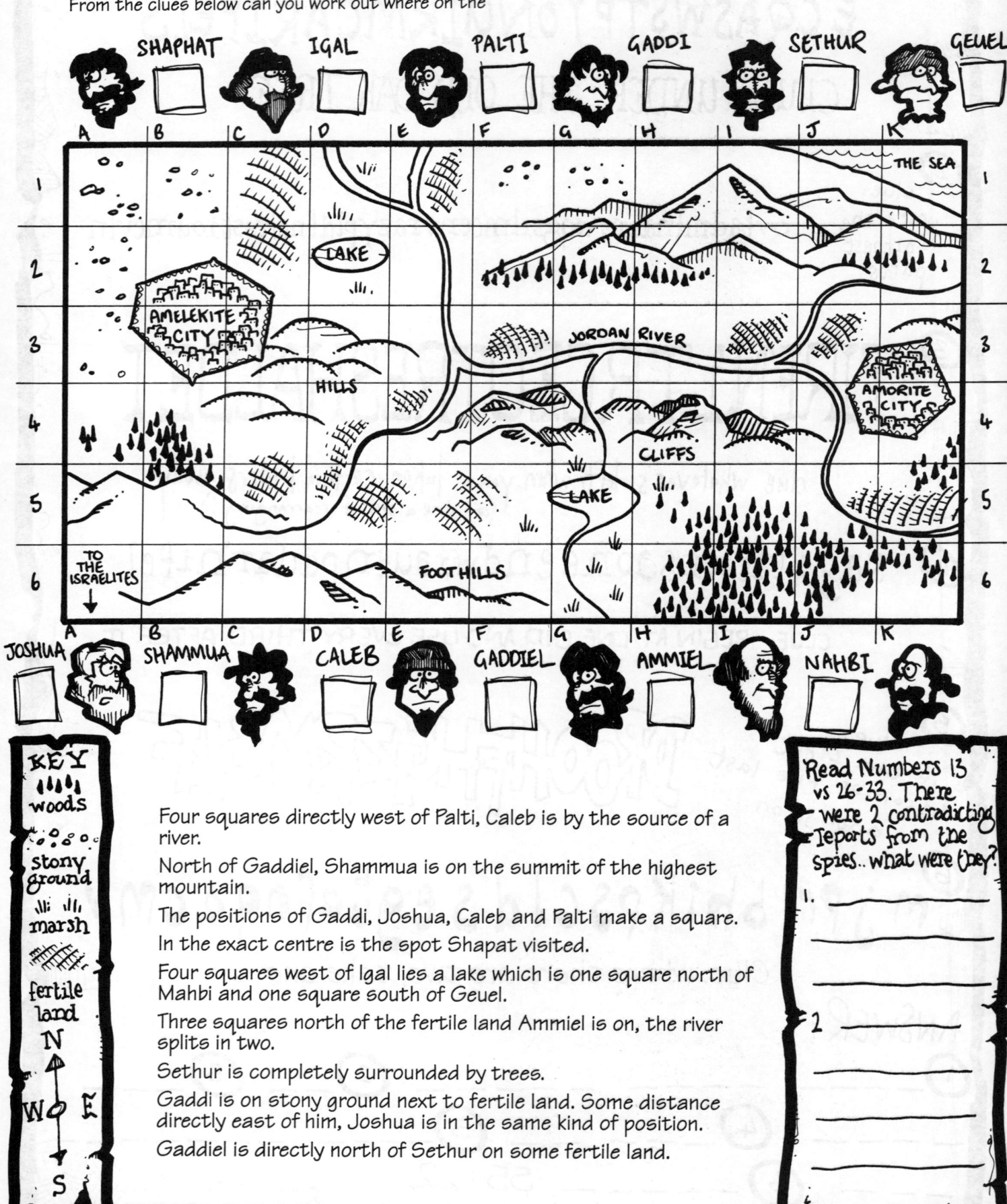

Four squares directly west of Palti, Caleb is by the source of a river.

North of Gaddiel, Shammua is on the summit of the highest mountain.

The positions of Gaddi, Joshua, Caleb and Palti make a square.

In the exact centre is the spot Shapat visited.

Four squares west of Igal lies a lake which is one square north of Mahbi and one square south of Geuel.

Three squares north of the fertile land Ammiel is on, the river splits in two.

Sethur is completely surrounded by trees.

Gaddi is on stony ground next to fertile land. Some distance directly east of him, Joshua is in the same kind of position.

Gaddiel is directly north of Sethur on some fertile land.

KEY

|||| woods

stony ground

marsh

fertile land

N
W   E
S

Read Numbers 13 vs 26-33. There were 2 contradicting reports from the spies.. what were they?

1. _____

2 _____

EPISODE 9

The Consequences of Sin

The Consequences of Sin

Background

When the twelve spies had returned from Canaan and given their report, the Israelites all began to complain. Instead of listening to Joshua and Caleb who gave a good report and urged them to trust God, they listened to the other spies who told tales about the strength of the people in the land. Moses and Aaron fell to their knees to pray and Joshua and Caleb urged the people not to anger God by distrust and unbelief, yet they persisted and God came down to the Tent of Meeting and spoke to them through Moses.

Reading

Numbers 14:28-34 and 20:1-13.

Overheads

1 (background) Joshua and Caleb urge the Israelites to faith.
2 (14:30) Moses speaks the words of God to the people.
3 (20:11) Moses strikes the rock.

What this episode tells us

What we can learn from Moses
The requirements of trust and the consequences of sin.

What we can learn about God
He requires a standard from us.

Discussion questions and desired answers

What have the Israelites done wrong in this episode?
They have distrusted God in his promise of providing a land for them and again complained against him.

What does God do?
He punishes them. They are to wander in the desert until everyone from that current generation (except Joshua and Caleb) is dead.

Moses and Aaron are also punished later on. What did they do wrong?
Moses struck the rock after God told him to speak to it and did not give the glory of the miracle to God.

Considering Moses' relationship with God, do you think his punishment (to not actually enter the Promised Land himself) seemed severe?
Possibly, but it was due to his having such an incredible relationship and privilege with God that God in turn expected such a high standard from him. 1 Corinthians 4:2 says, 'Those who have been given a trust must prove faithful.' The more God gives the greater responsibility there is.

Does God punish us too, when we sin?
No he doesn't. We have seen how punishment came as a result of breaking the law. Now that we live by grace we are able to be forgiven.

Does forgiveness therefore mean that we can expect no consequences from sinning?

Not at all. If we, for example, steal something from a shop and genuinely regret it, God will forgive us but it doesn't necessarily mean the police wouldn't get called or that we would not get a criminal record! Sometimes we need to live through the consequences of our actions.

In Moses' day it was obvious if someone sinned because they had the law that told them what was forbidden. How do we as Christians know when we sin?

As Christians the Holy Spirit lives inside us and will show us our sin. This is called conviction. Sin is just a word used to describe anything we do that isn't what God would want. It could be attitudes, words or deeds. Jesus tells us the Holy Spirit will bring conviction (John 16:7-11), i.e. make us aware of the wrong.

Read Hebrews 12:10-11. What can we expect if we ignore conviction?
God to discipline us.

What is the difference between punishment and discipline?
Punishment is a consequence but discipline is for our benefit, to correct and teach and guide. God might allow us to pass through a situation where we recognise a wrong we'd previously ignored. It might not be a pleasant situation but if we'd not ignored the wrong we wouldn't have experienced it.

Living under grace as we do, we need not fear punishment or discipline (which is for our benefit) but should remember that we still have a requirement on us to live as God would want. If we don't there could be conviction and even discipline – the consequences of sin.

Additional material

Further reading

The story of David and Bathsheba (2 Samuel 11). Although David's sins are forgiven him, the consequences of his sin (death of their first son and constant violence in his household) remain.

Worksheet

Self-explanatory.

Take-home sheet

Identical squares: H2 and L6, M1 and I3, N6 and B5, C1 and H6.

Closing prayer

Dear God, thank you for the life you have given me; that I can live knowing you don't look to punish me whenever I make a mistake. Thank you also that in your love you have given the Holy Spirit to live inside me and show me if I displease you. Help me to hear and pay attention to the Spirit and to understand that your ways are the very best for me. Amen.

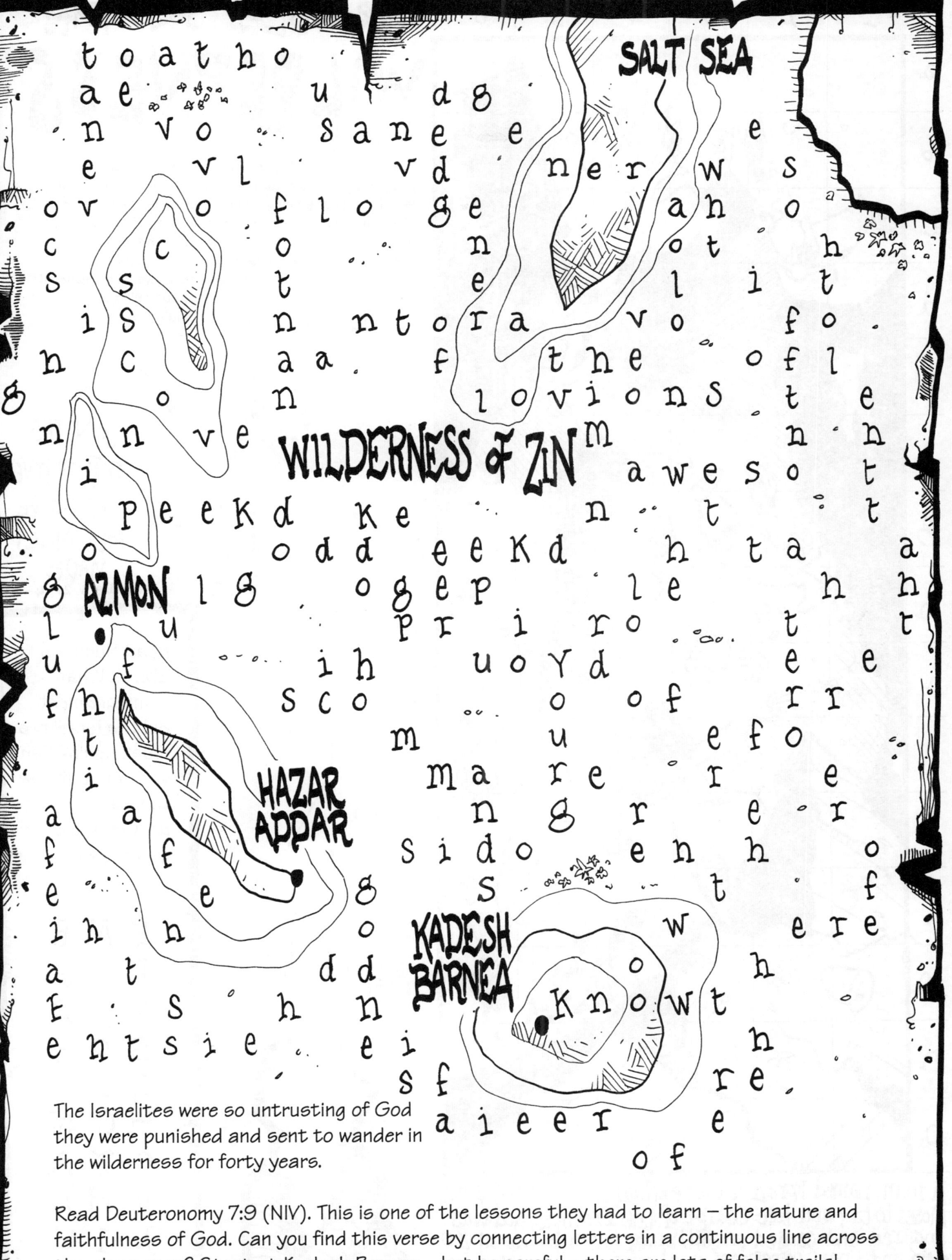

SALT SEA

WILDERNESS OF ZIN

AZMON

HAZAR ADDAR

KADESH BARNEA

The Israelites were so untrusting of God they were punished and sent to wander in the wilderness for forty years.

Read Deuteronomy 7:9 (NIV). This is one of the lessons they had to learn — the nature and faithfulness of God. Can you find this verse by connecting letters in a continuous line across the above map? Start at Kadesh Barnea — but be careful — there are lots of false trails!

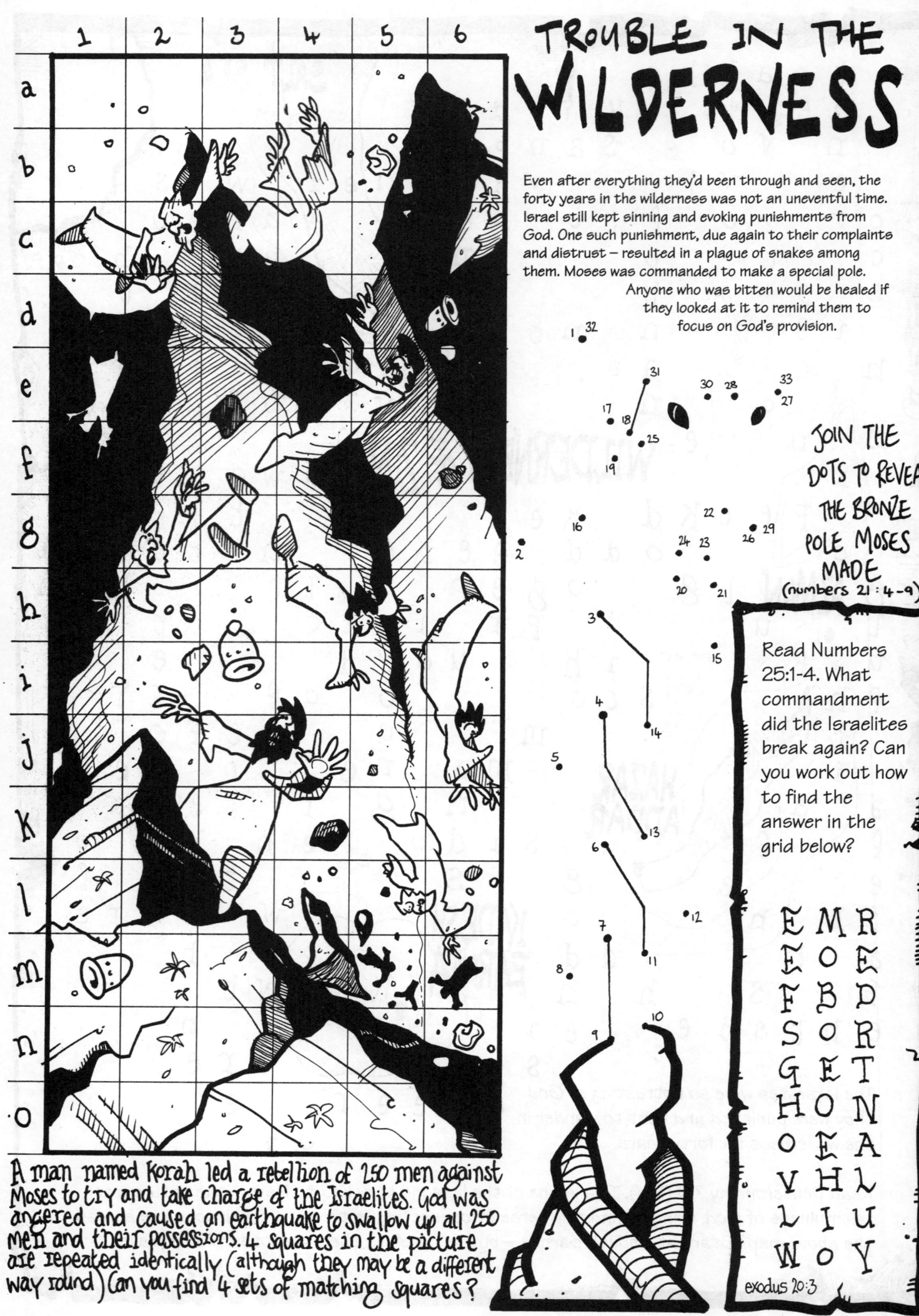

TROUBLE IN THE WILDERNESS

Even after everything they'd been through and seen, the forty years in the wilderness was not an uneventful time. Israel still kept sinning and evoking punishments from God. One such punishment, due again to their complaints and distrust – resulted in a plague of snakes among them. Moses was commanded to make a special pole. Anyone who was bitten would be healed if they looked at it to remind them to focus on God's provision.

JOIN THE DOTS TO REVEAL THE BRONZE POLE MOSES MADE
(numbers 21 : 4-9)

Read Numbers 25:1-4. What commandment did the Israelites break again? Can you work out how to find the answer in the grid below?

exodus 20:3

A man named Korah led a rebellion of 250 men against Moses to try and take charge of the Israelites. God was angered and caused an earthquake to swallow up all 250 men and their possessions. 4 squares in the picture are repeated identically (although they may be a different way round) Can you find 4 sets of matching squares?

EPISODE 10

The Promised Land

EPISODE 10

The Promised Land

Background

For forty years the Israelites wandered in the wilderness, as God had said. In time, the generation who disbelieved God, died, leaving their children as the ones who would enter the Promised Land. Aaron also died and from that moment the people began their journey back to Canaan. Moses still could not enter the land so before the Israelites did he spoke to them all.

Reading

Deuteronomy 4:9-14, 32-40; 34:1-8.

Overheads

1 (background) The Israelites in the wilderness.
2 (4:14) Moses speaks to the people.
3 (34:1) Moses sees the Promised Land.

What this episode tells us

What we can learn from Moses
We will build faith by remembering God's faithfulness and provision.

What we can learn about God
He is faithful to us and to his word.

Discussion questions and desired answers

These chapters are Moses' final words to the Israelites. What would you say the emphasis of his message is?
To remember all of their past experiences and to think of their present and future situation, i.e. they were about to enter the land God had promised.

Why do you think that's important for them?
Time and time again we've seen Israel not trusting and disbelieving God. By accurately remembering God's faithfulness they would not have any reason to distrust him.

Take time out here for a practical example: pick one person and ask them to tell any other child one simple fact, e.g. what they ate for breakfast. Ask that child what the first said in a conversation similar to this:
> 'Cornflakes.'
> 'I don't believe her/him. Do you?'
> 'Yes.'
> 'Would you say you're convinced it's true?'
> 'Maybe.'
> 'What if I said I spoke to them beforehand and told them what I was going to ask and told them to lie. Are you convinced 100 per cent it's true now?'

And so on, the point being they can't be 100 per cent sure. Then ask them the same question:
> 'What did you have?'
> 'Ricicles.'
> 'I don't believe you.'

Etc. Ask them eventually if they doubted the first person, then whether or not your disbelief of something they *know* happened caused them to doubt it in any way. Why not?

How do you think this is relevant to the Israelites and to us?
Just as God did fantastic things for the Israelites so also we have experience of God, answers to prayer, blessings, etc. When something has happened to us no one can take the actual experience away from us. We'll always know it's true. With God, the more we experience of him the more confident in him and in his word, his promises, etc, we can be.

Is it just other people disbelieving that can cause us to doubt?
No. Situations or problems, uncertainties and doubts can all cause us to doubt God or our experiences.

How can we make sure we do not doubt?
By truly experiencing and recognising God or his provision in our lives, as Moses urged the Israelites to do, and then by always remembering such things, as well as always seeking new ones. Perhaps if you forget things easily it would be good to keep a diary of the times God answers your prayers or touches you in some way. If ever you feel uncertain you can read over it to remind yourself of God's faithful and loving nature. The worksheet today is a cover for just such a book. Put your name on it and perhaps draw something on the cover.

Additional material

Fun

'I Spy With My Moses Eye!' Group Game. Select one person to be Moses who must 'climb to view the promised land' or find something high to sit or stand on (be careful though!) All the other children must sit on the floor and 'Moses' chooses something he can see from his vantage point but they can't. Then an eye-spy-style game takes place. Moses may answer 'yes' or 'no' to questions if guessing proves to be difficult.

Further reading

Joshua 4:4-9. Having crossed the Jordan on dry ground into the Promised Land God commands Joshua to make a stone memorial that will always remind the people of that occasion and of God's faithfulness and provision.

Worksheet

Self-explanatory.

Take-home sheet

Self-explanatory.

Closing prayer

Dear Father God, thank you for everything you've ever done for me and blessed me with. Help me not to forget such things so that I won't ever forget your true nature and care for me. I pray also, Lord, that you will continue to bless me and show me even greater things so that not only will I remember and thank you for the past but I will enjoy the present and look forward to the future. Thank you, Lord. Amen.

The Promised Land

Some of Moses' last words were a song declaring the virtues of God. Part of the song is below, taken from Deuteronomy 32:3-4 (NIV). Can you find the missing words in the grid on the right?

'I will _____ the _____ of the Lord. Oh, _____ the _____ of our God! He is the _____, his _____ are _____, and all his ways are _____. A _____ God who does no _____, _____ and _____ is he.'

```
R E F W O R K S H L M R B R W C Y H
N M I M V X B F A I T H F U L X V T
H A L S S E N T A E R G E T M R U C
B N E K Y K F L I N O U Y S C L S E
O C G U C Z C E S W V X D U I N T F
J A S P W O A O M P J F Z J G A O R
D G N O R W D G R K T A E H K P R E
Q T U P R I G H T Q W I Q Z S A T P
```

— Read the last verses of Deuteronomy (34:10-12) to conclude the story of Moses

God is Good to me

THE PERSONAL DIARY OF

Before finally moving into the promised land Moses stood and spoke to the children of Israel. He reminded them of everything God had done to bring them to this point – of his faithfulness, miracles and answers to prayer.

Sometimes it's all too easy to forget the things God has done for us. As time goes by the details become hazy and unclear – if we're not careful we can forget altogether!

This then, is a personal diary of the things God has done for me, blessed me with and shown me, So I can always look at it and remember how good, trustworthy and faithful God is to me....

EPISODE 11

What We Have Learned from Moses

What We Have Learned from Moses

Lesson summary

This lesson is a review of what has been covered in the previous episodes, with extra game and worksheet pages instead of the usual overheads.

Discussion questions and desired answers

Once even Aaron challenged Moses' leadership. Moses didn't defend himself because God chose to do it. Read Numbers 12:6-8. What does God call Moses?

Faithful in all his house, and his servant.

God was very pleased with Moses. Looking back over his life, what aspects of his character stand out and how do they relate to us; in particular, his faithfulness?

Moses was consistently faithful and obedient to the things God told him. God doesn't necessarily tell us what to do every day. Being faithful also means living as God would desire us to, not just obeying his specific direction. Faithfulness to God and to his ways is something we can see in Moses and something God wants to be able to see in us.

Trust?

Moses is always seen trusting and believing God, in complete contrast to the Israelites who were always doubting and disbelieving and constantly angering God. We can see that God never let Moses down and deciding if we'd rather be like Moses or the Israelites shouldn't be hard!

Desire for God?

We have seen the amazing relationship Moses had with God and his desire to want even more, then the fact that God granted that request. If we, like Moses, desire to know and love God better we can be sure he will not let us down.

Fearing God?

To fear God does not mean we are frightened of him, but rather we recognise his complete nature and what he deserves. As well as being a friend and a father to us he is a holy and awesome God who we are not worthy to come to. It is only through Jesus we are able to be made acceptable to God's holy standard.

We have seen how law has been replaced by grace. How is God's grace shown to us?

God, having demonstrated through the law man's unworthiness and his holiness, gave Jesus to take the punishment of law in our place, so that through his grace – that which we do not deserve – we can have relationship with him.

How was God's grace shown to Israel?

Israel was always God's chosen nation, chosen through nothing they had done or deserved to be the nation Jesus would come out of. God constantly protects and cares for Israel, even when her people complain against him.

How can we see God's faithfulness in this?

God brought Israel to the land he had promised them, just as he said he would. He did everything he promised for them. This is just one occurrence in scripture where God is faithful. There are so many more because it is God's nature. Faithfulness is an attribute of God. That means something he literally is and by his very nature can be nothing less than 100 per cent in that area. God is faithful to us and to his words and promises.

What should we never forget from the story of Moses about God's words and promises?

They are true – all of them! God's word is true and to be believed when he speaks to us as individuals or as the whole world. God loves you and that's just one promise that is true. Isn't that great!

Additional material

Fun

'Pick a Scene' Game. Give the children some time to pick a scene from the story of Moses and act it out – either as a presentation to the rest of the group or as a 'guess which scene' style game. If relevant, perhaps a section could be rehearsed and performed to the church.

Worksheet

'True or False' Game. This can be read out by the teacher in lesson time. Keep score as you go, give all eighteen questions then go over the answers.

One worksheet is an empty 'Stone Tablet' (page 91). It is for the children to draw a picture of their favourite scene from the Moses story. You may like to make this into a competition, giving prizes for the best drawings or possibly display them in church when finished so that everyone can see what the youth group have been doing. Use the box to write what the scene is and why it is their favourite.

Take-home sheet

This week's take-home sheet is a board game, First To Canaan, pages 92-95. Alternatively it could be played in lesson time, if relevant.

Closing prayer

Dear Father God, thank you for all I have learnt from the story of Moses and about you. Please help me, Father, to remember these lessons and to use them to improve my relationship with, and understanding of, you. Thank you for your Son, Jesus – please give me a greater understanding of what Jesus has done for me and how I can show my thankfulness. Amen.

Moses – True or False

Warning!
Not every subject here has been covered in the teachings
and some of the questions are subtle, so listen and guess carefully!

1. God guided the Israelites as a pillar of fire by day and a pillar of cloud by night. (False – it was the other way round.)

2. Aaron was Moses' elder cousin. (False – he was Moses' brother.)

3. At a place called Marah the water was too bitter to drink. God showed Moses a piece of wood which, when thrown into the water, turned the water sweet. (True.)

4. Once, when Moses was disheartened, God sent a wild bear to comfort him. (Very false!)

5. Moses melted the Israelites' golden calf and made them drink it with water. (True.)

6. The spies sent into Canaan returned with a bunch of grapes so large it took two men to carry it. (True.)

7. In front of Pharaoh both Aaron and the Egyptian magicians turned their staffs into snakes but Aaron's staff ate up all the others. (True.)

8. When the Israelites complained of hunger, God provided something called Manna for them to eat. It was a bread-like substance that grew out of the ground. (False – Manna fell like dew.)

9. When the Israelites were being bitten by snakes in the desert God told Moses to make a bronze snake on a pole. Anyone who looked at the bronze snake was healed. (True.)

10. God sent eleven plagues against Pharaoh, the last of which was the death of all Egyptian first-born. (False – there were only ten plagues.)

11. When Moses had spoken face to face with God, his face would shine so brightly that he had to put a veil over it. (True.)

12. Once the Israelites disputed that Aaron was God's chosen leader. To prove it, God caused Aaron's staff to sprout flowers and grow fruit. (True.)

13. In the Passover the Israelites had to hang a lamb outside their houses. The angel of death would see the lamb and pass the house by. (False – it was blood on the doorways that saved them.)

14. The Israelites were to gather Manna fresh every morning. If they tried to save the previous day's Manna it became full of maggots and stank. (True.)

15. During a battle once, the Israelites were only winning when Moses had his arms held up. When he became tired, two people had to hold his arms up for him. (True.)

16. When the Israelites left Egypt God caused the Egyptians to look favourably on them and give them gold, silver and clothing. (True.)

17. During the forty years Israel wandered in the wilderness they were in many battles. It was in one of these battles Aaron was killed. (False – Aaron did not die in battle.)

18. When the Egyptian army was chasing the Israelites through the Red Sea, God caused the wheels of their chariots to fall off to slow them down. (True.)

First to Canaan
Game for two or more players

How to play

You will need

One dice. Counters (such as coins or buttons.) Letter cards enough for every player. (Alternatively a pen and paper each to keep track of letters collected/lost.)

Object of the game

Each player is an Israelite having to wander in the desert until it is time for God's Promised Land – the land of Canaan – to be entered. Be the first Israelite to enter by collecting the letters to spell PROMISE and getting to Canaan.

Moving

Depending on which colour square you roll on, moving changes as follows:

White – move the total thrown either North, South, East or West.

Grey – as above but double the amount thrown.

(So far you do not have to move in a continuous line – you may change direction but *must* use up your total number achieved without retracing your steps on that turn.)

Black – move continuously in one of the directions below that corresponds to the number of your roll:

1 either North or South.

2 either South-west or North-east.

3 either East or West.

4 either North-west or South-east.

5 either South or North-east.

6 either North or South-west.

In the event that your number rolled leads you into a rock, you may stop!

Letters

Letters are collected by landing on the letter squares (not by passing over them). Letters do not have to be collected in order but you must possess all seven letters of 'promise' and no more, in order to enter Canaan.

Other players

If you land exactly on the same square as another player then you receive one letter from them. However, you do not choose which letter – they do! Consequently, deliberate collisions are a risk as you may receive a letter you'll then need to get rid of! For this reason, it is best to keep your collected letters hidden. To get rid of extra letters either give them (one at a time!) to players who collide with you, *or* land on any letter square and lose a letter instead of receiving one.

In the event that two players collide on a letter circle, then the second player to land there first receives or loses a letter from the circle then receives one from the other player.

The more people playing the more collisions are likely to happen and the harder the game becomes!

May the Israelite who finally takes hold of God's promise enter the land first!

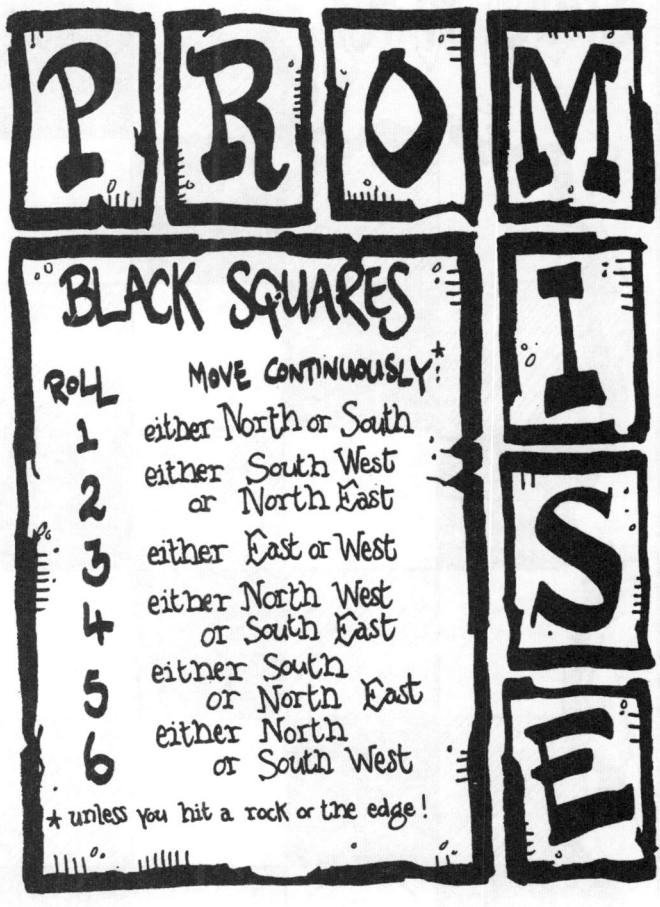

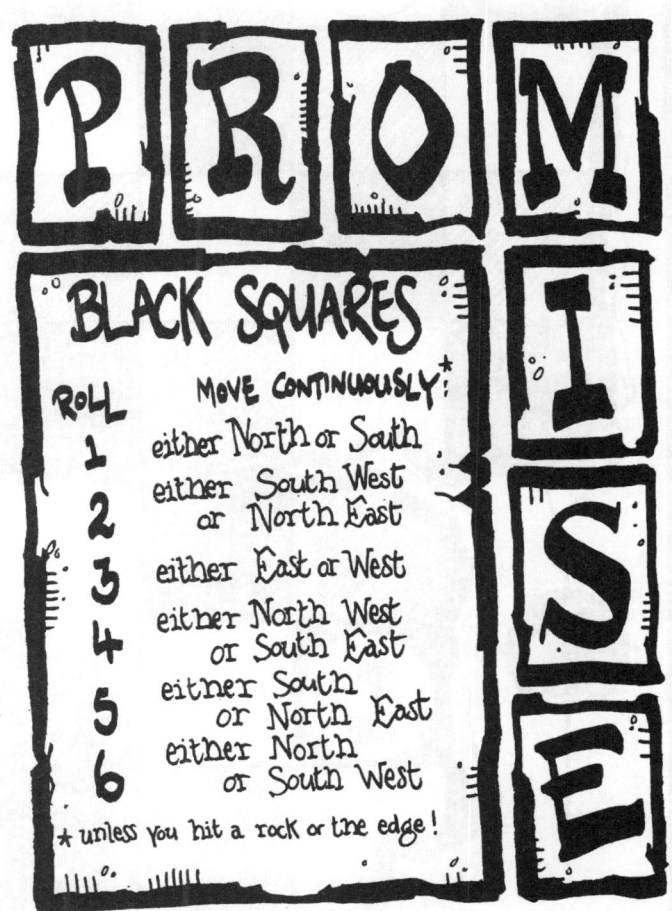

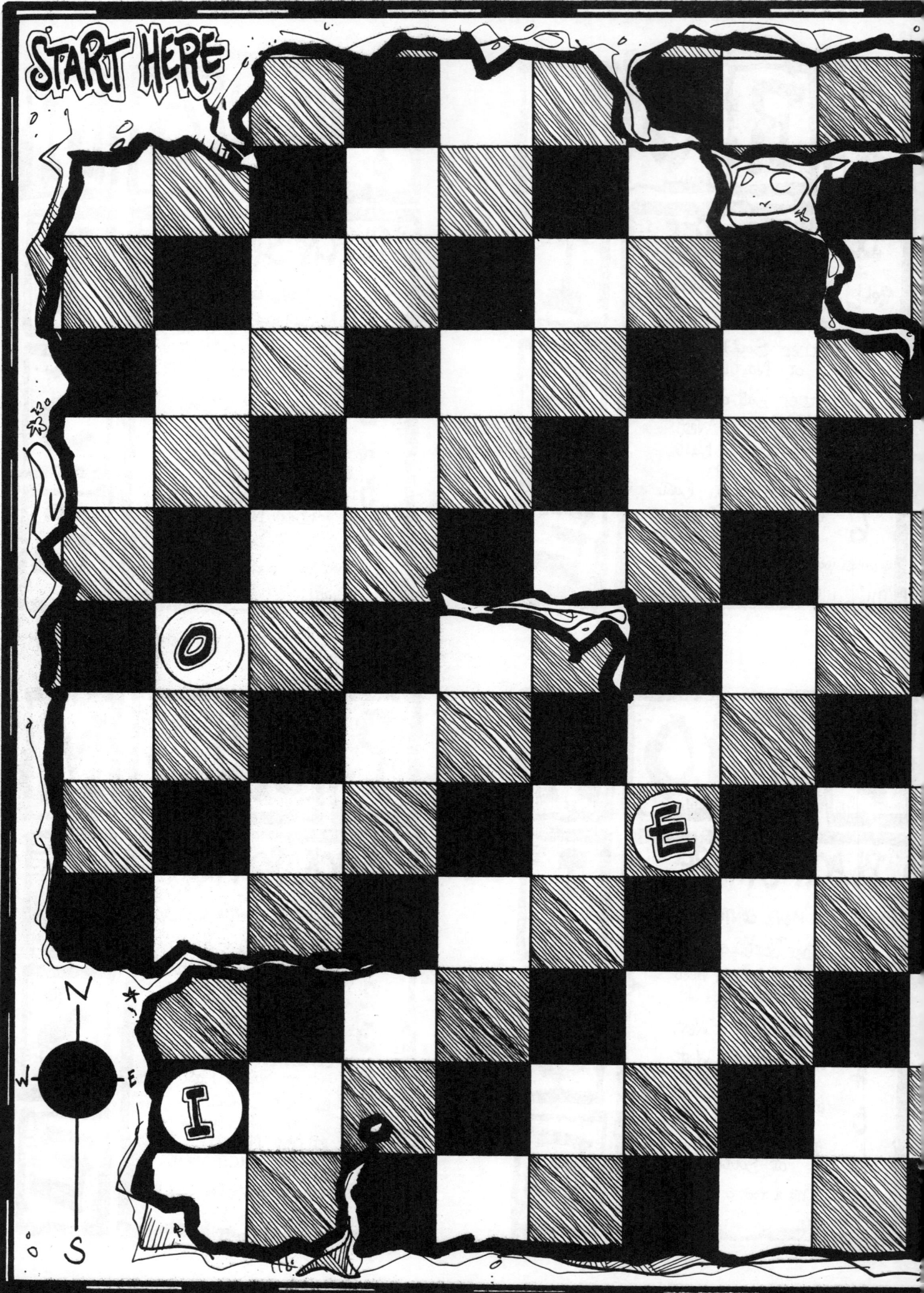

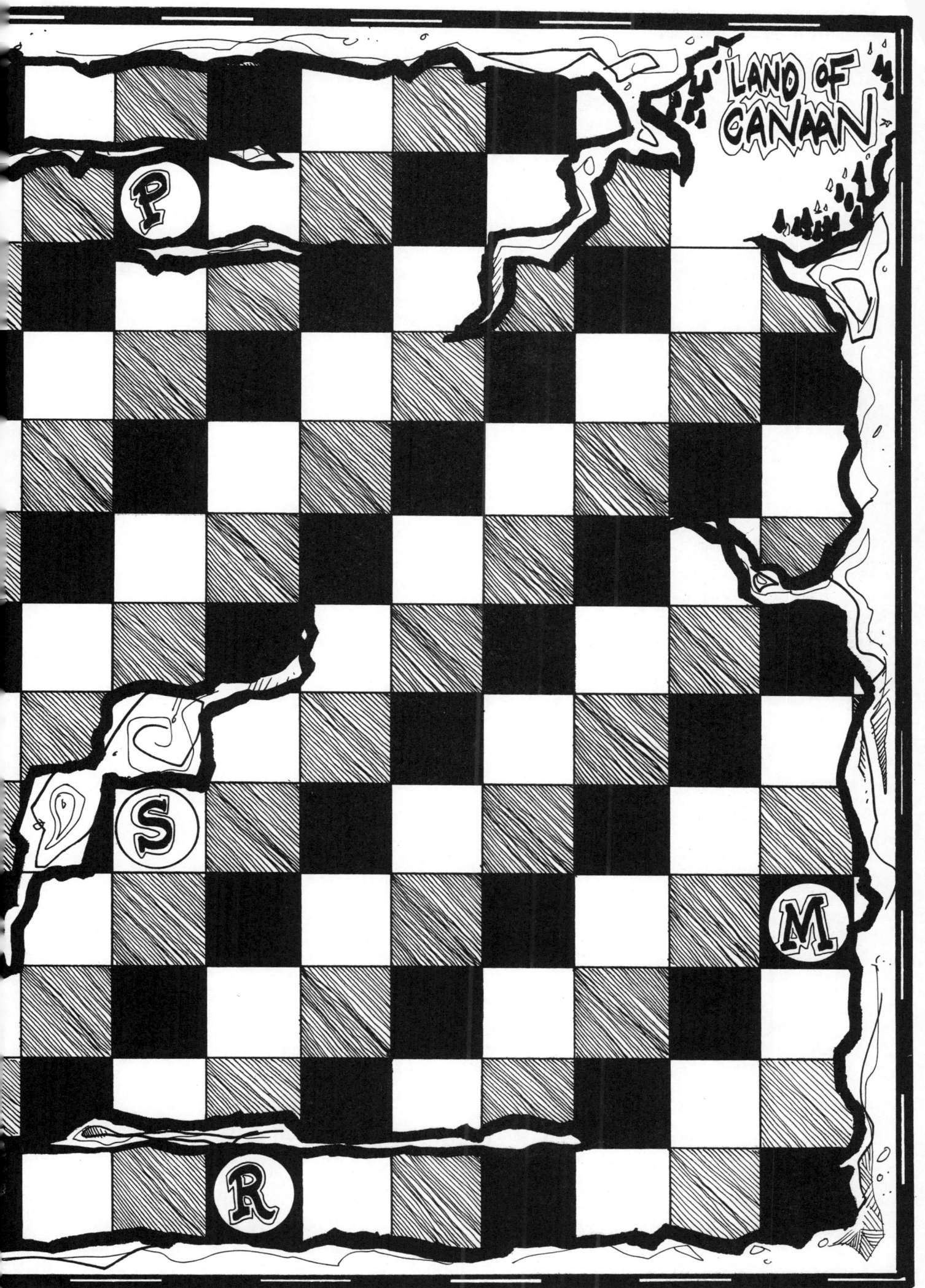